O.J.

O.J.

by Bill Gutman

**tempo
books**

GROSSET & DUNLAP, INC.
Publishers   New York

ACKNOWLEDGMENTS

The author wishes to thank the following people for their help in supplying background and photographic material for this book:

Joe Browne and Kay O'Reilly of the National Football League office; Don Phinney of the Buffalo Bills; Judy Lake of the University of Southern California sports information department; Frank Yohan; and Robert L. Smith, a fine photographer who had the good fortune to follow O.J. on his record-breaking trek.

Picture Credits: Buffalo Bills, pages 44, 70, 75, 76, 89; Robert L. Smith, pages 8, 37, 48, 53, 54, 55, 58, 61, 64–65, 76 (bottom), 79, 81, 82, 85, 86–87, 90, 91, 93; Wide World, pages 13, 21, 24, 27, 29.

CONTENTS

For Beth, a record-breaker herself

CHAPTER 1

Breaking records is not new to O.J. Simpson. He has been doing it ever since he began playing football. He has always wanted to be the best.

In 1973, O.J. Simpson was the very best. He had one of the greatest record-breaking seasons a running back has ever had. No one could stop him. The teams playing against O.J.'s Buffalo Bills knew O.J. was going to get the football. They were ready. But they still couldn't stop him.

When the season ended, everyone in football was talking about the man they call "The Juice!" He had run for more yards in one season than any player in National Football League history. His final record was 2,003 yards on 332 carries. The number of carries was a record, too. He had also gained more than 200 yards a game in three games and more than 100 yards each in 11 games. Both were new records. And the Bills, led by O.J., broke the Miami Dolphins' record for most rushing yards in a season.

It was a great year. Once again, people were saying that O.J. was the best. They started saying it when he played college ball at the University of Southern California. He broke a lot of records then, too. Everyone knew about him. After each game, people all over the country would ask:

"How many yards did O.J. get?"

When he came into the NFL, people thought he'd keep breaking records.

But O.J. joined the Buffalo Bills. Buffalo was not a good team, then. The team did not have many star players. The blocking was very poor. O.J. had to run on his own. And the team was often behind. They had to pass the ball to try to catch up. It was like a bad dream. Suddenly, O.J. wasn't a star. He was just another runner, trying hard to get yards. But without good blockers he was often hit hard. He gained very little.

It was a bad time for O.J., but he was used to hard years. He'd known them before, especially in his early days.

Orenthal James Simpson was born on July 9, 1947, in the Potrero Hills neighborhood of San Francisco, California. Almost everybody who lived in Potrero Hills was black. The neighborhood was very old and most of the people were poor. Many people said Potrero Hills was fast becoming a ghetto neighborhood.

It was easy for young boys to get into trouble in Potrero Hills. O.J.'s mother worked at a hospital to support her four children and young O.J. was often on his own out on the streets.

O.J. didn't think much about what he'd do when he grew up. He was more worried about having enough money for the next meal. But his mother worked very hard and the family always seemed to make ends meet.

O.J. didn't think seriously about sports then either. O.J.'s cousin was baseball star Ernie Banks. O.J.'s mother used to tell him how much sports did for Ernie. But young O.J. was more interested in running with his friends on the street.

"We really had no one to control us

At USC, football wasn't the only thing O.J. worked at.

then," O.J. recalls. "When we started getting into trouble there was no one there to tell us what might happen. I guess those of us who stayed out of real big trouble were just lucky."

O.J. didn't play much during his elementary and junior high school days. He just fooled around with football, baseball and basketball when there was nothing better to do. It wasn't until he reached Galileo High School that he finally started to play for real.

Galileo was near the Chinatown section of San Francisco. Most of the students at the school were Chinese. Oriental youngsters aren't usually as big as American children. So O.J. and his friend, Al Cowlings, were just about the biggest kids in the school. O.J. stood 5–10 and weighed 160 pounds then. Cowlings was about the same, maybe a little bigger. The rest of the kids were small.

That made O.J. and Cowlings the stars of the team. O.J. started out as a tackle on the football team because he was so big. But one day his coach, Jack McBride, saw him carry the ball in practice. That did it. O.J. moved as if he'd been a runner all his life. So the coach made him a back. But his first two years the team didn't win a single game.

"It wasn't really fun then," says O.J.'s friend, Al Cowlings. "The other guys didn't really know how to play. I was O.J.'s blocker. I opened the holes and he ran through them."

O.J. played baseball, too. He was a catcher and a good one. But he broke his hand his sophomore year and didn't play baseball any more. He liked football a lot better.

Football was slowly becoming very important to O.J. He liked carrying that ball, breaking away for his long runs. But he still liked going to parties and fooling around. School came last. Only football kept him from dropping out.

"School didn't really mean much," says O.J. "We were always getting into some kind of trouble. We were sent to the dean's office all the time. Sometimes we cut classes or were caught smoking, stuff like that. If it wasn't for football I don't think we would have come to school at all."

Then O.J. started working at the Booker T. Washington Community Center. It was a place that helped younger boys to stay out of trouble. And in helping the younger boys, O.J. stayed out of trouble, too. He met a girl there named Marguerite Whitley. She and O.J. began dating. She helped him a great deal and they were finally married.

"It was the first time in my life that I really had something to do," O.J. remembers. "I was busy all the time and didn't have time to mess around. That's when I finally started thinking about the future. I knew I wanted my high school diploma and I even thought about going to college for the first time."

O.J. got his diploma, all right. The football team had even won five games that year and many colleges knew that O.J. was becoming a fine runner. But he had not done his schoolwork for such a long time that his grades at Galileo High weren't good enough for college. So O.J. had to go to a junior college to try to get better grades. In the fall of 1965 he began at City College of San Francisco.

CHAPTER 2

At City College, O.J. started making headlines. In his very first game he was a star. He was a fast, strong runner with good "moves." He could get away from tacklers many different ways. And when he was hit he always dragged them a few more yards before going down.

In one game against San Jose City College, O.J. ran for six touchdowns. More people than ever were beginning to realize how good he was. When the year ended he had gained more than 1,000 yards. He ran for nearly 10 yards every time he carried the ball. And he had scored 26 touchdowns. Now the big colleges wanted him. His grades were up and they began asking him to come to their schools.

It isn't easy for a youngster like O.J. to decide on a college. Everyone makes promises. Some schools keep the promises, and some don't. Some colleges just want to win their games. They are looking for ballplayers, and sometimes they don't care whether the player gets an education or not. It's a sad fact, but true. O.J. knew this. He wanted to be very careful about the college he went to.

He visited several colleges, places like Arizona State and Utah. But he really wanted to stay in California and go to USC. And to go there he needed some more courses at City College. So

O.J. decided to stay at City College for another year.

It was a good choice. He got more experience. He ran for another 1,000 yards and scored 28 touchdowns. He also studied hard and got the grades he needed. Then he announced he'd be going to the University of Southern California for the 1967 season.

"I felt USC was the best place for me," said O.J. "I only had two years of varsity ball left and I wanted to make my mark. USC had many great runners. Mike Garrett was the last one and he set a lot of records. If I went to USC I could put myself up against Mike's records. And then I thought I'd have a good chance to win the Heisman Trophy. I wanted that very badly, too."

The Heisman Trophy is given to the best college player of the year.

O.J. was a track runner too. He shows his speed here by winning his heat in the 100 meter dash at the Track and Field Championships in 1968.

O.J. wanted to be the best and he was willing to work for it.

The USC teams were called "Trojans." O.J. was a track runner for the Trojans as well as a football player. But football always came first. When the football season started Coach John McKay gave O.J. number "32." He made him the starting tailback. And O.J. took off.

He was great right from the beginning. In his very first game, against Washington State, he ran for more than 100 yards. Everyone around USC knew he was someone very special right then and there.

A week later he showed how strong he was. Playing against big, tough Notre Dame, O.J. carried again and again. He would carry the ball five, six, or seven times in a row and he didn't seem to get tired. When the game ended O.J. was over 100 yards

again and USC had won, 24–7. Someone then asked him how he could
carry the ball so much.

"I'd hear the quarterback call my
number," O.J. answered, "and I'd say
to myself, 'Lord, not again!' But once
I got the ball my instincts took over
and my legs did the rest of the work."

O.J.'s legs did a lot of work that
year. Playing against the University of
Washington he ran for 235 yards and
carried the ball 30 times. He hurt his
foot in the game against Oregon University, but a week later ran for 188
yards against Oregon State U. By then
everyone knew about O.J. He was becoming one of the most well-known
players in the country. People always
wanted to know how many yards he
gained.

USC's final game that year was
against UCLA. Both California
schools wanted to go to the Rose

O.J. always keeps his legs in great shape. At USC he rode a bicycle to class to get a little more exercise.

Bowl. The winning team would go. UCLA had a star quarterback named Gary Beban. It looked as if either Beban or O.J. would win the Heisman Trophy. So it was a big game for both players. More than 90,000 people came to the Los Angeles Coliseum. The game was also on national television. The whole country would be watching.

The UCLA defense wanted to stop O.J. They didn't want him to break away for one of his long runs. They knew he'd be sure to gain some yards, maybe five or ten, but they ganged up to keep him from getting 20 or 30.

At the same time, Beban was calling a good game. He was a rollout quarterback who ran to his right or left. Then he could either keep the ball, or pitch it to another back. Or he could stop and throw. He did everything well and was a good leader. Early in the fourth period he had his team ahead, 20–14.

O.J. was not having one of his best days. He had gained around 100 yards, but he hadn't "broken" one yet. The UCLA defense was holding him to short gains, just as they had planned. They were also tackling him very hard. The last couple of times he was tackled O.J. got up very slowly. It looked as if he was getting very tired.

Late in the game, with UCLA ahead, 20–14, the Trojans got the ball again. There wasn't much time left. If they didn't do it now, UCLA would win the game. They moved the ball to their own 36-yard line. Quarterback Steve Sogge wanted to keep the drive going. He called an off-tackle play for O.J. It was the kind of play that usually gets about six to ten yards. That was all Sogge expected.

Sogge took the snap, whirled

O.J. was a star from the first time he put
on uniform number 32 for the University
of Southern California.

around, and handed it to O.J. as he sped past. O.J. burst through a hole in the line. In front of him were three UCLA tacklers, ready to stop him. It was the same thing O.J. had faced all afternoon. But this time he didn't run into them and settle for a nice gain. Instead, he cut sharply to his right. He did it so quickly that the three defenders were left grabbing at air.

Once he was around them he really turned on the speed. Everyone thought he was too tired to run like that. But they learned that O.J. always had enough for an extra effort. He outran two other defenders toward the sideline, then he cut back to the middle of the field. No one could catch him. He ran into the end zone for a 64-yard touchdown run! The game was tied at 20–20. The kick for the extra point was good. USC had

The end of a 15-yard touchdown run against North-western. For two seasons, O.J. was the greatest running back college football has ever known.

won, 21–20. They had a 9–1 season and would go to the Rose Bowl.

O.J. finished the UCLA game with 177 yards. That gave him 1,543 for the season. He had carried the ball 291 times. He was on every all-America team. He was the best runner in the country.

"O.J.'s run against UCLA was the best I've ever seen," one college coach said. "He made a 90-degree cut after going through the line and he didn't lose a step of his speed. I didn't think any man could do that. I haven't seen every runner, but O.J. is the best of those I've watched in my time."

In spite of his great play, O.J. didn't win the Heisman Trophy that year. Beban did. Most football people said O.J. had a better year, but Beban had been good for three years. O.J. was disappointed, but he knew he could try again in 1968.

The Rose Bowl game was a second disappointment. USC lost to Purdue, 14–13. But the whole team looked to the next year. There was really something to work for.

CHAPTER 3

The first game of the 1968 season was against the University of Minnesota. Like everyone else, the Gophers wanted to stop O.J. And like everyone else, they couldn't.

O.J. scored two times in the first half. On one play he ran for a 36-yard touchdown, twisting and turning, getting away from every player who tried to tackle him. But Minnesota had the lead and they held it. It was more of the same in the third period. O.J. kept running, but his team was losing.

In the fourth period the score was

20–16 in favor of Minnesota. There were just minutes left in the game. USC had the ball on the Minnesota 45-yard line. Quarterback Sogge didn't want to take any chances. He did just one thing. He kept giving the ball to O.J.

Six times in a row O.J. carried the ball. And the Gophers couldn't stop him. The sixth carry took him into the end zone. USC had a touchdown and the lead. In the final seconds of the game O.J. scored another touchdown, and USC won the game, 29–20.

It was a great start for the man they called "Orange Juice" (for O.J.). He had carried the ball 39 times. Not many players are strong enough to do that. And he gained 236 yards rushing. He also caught six passes for 59 yards. That meant he had gained almost 300 yards all by himself. He let people know from the first game that he was the best college player in the country.

After the game, O.J. talked about the beating a running back takes when he carries so many times.

"The night after a game the bumps and bruises really begin to hurt," he said. "Sometimes my wife and I go out to a party or movie, just to forget the game. But when I get home I'm up half the night. I don't want to go to bed because the mental tension and physical pain won't let me sleep. Every way I turn, it hurts. And the next day is always worse."

But O.J. ran and ran. He ran whenever quarterback Sogge called his number. He never complained. Even when he was hurt, he ran. Week after week he did his thing. He piled up the yards and led his team to victory.

"He's a fantastic young man," said his coach, John Mc Kay. "He runs as often as we need him to run, and the more he runs, the better he gets."

Things couldn't have been better for O.J. in 1968. His team didn't lose a single game. They were named the best team in the nation. As for O.J., he ran for 1,880 yards on 383 carries. Both were records at that time. He also scored 23 touchdowns.

When he went to USC, O.J. wanted to see if he could break some of Mike Garrett's records. He did, all right. He broke *all* of Garrett's records. He gained 3,423 yards on 674 carries. That was better than Garrett. And O.J. did it in just two years. It took Garrett three. And Garrett was a Heisman Trophy winner and pro star.

In December, O.J. reached another goal. He won the Heisman Trophy as the best college player in the land. A month later he scored two touchdowns in the Rose Bowl game, and USC won by a 14–3 score over Indiana. It was a triumphant end to the most brilliant college career ever. Now O.J. had to think about the future once more.

It looked like a rich future. Everyone wanted O.J. They wanted him to say he used their products. They wanted him to do television commercials. They wanted him as a sports announcer. They wanted him to speak at their dinners. He was not only a great football player, he was handsome and very smart. He was cool and had a sense of humor. And he could speak very well. So everyone wanted him. And of course the professional football teams wanted him most of all.

While he waited for the pro draft, O.J. could decide for himself what

When you're a big star, someone always wants to talk with you.

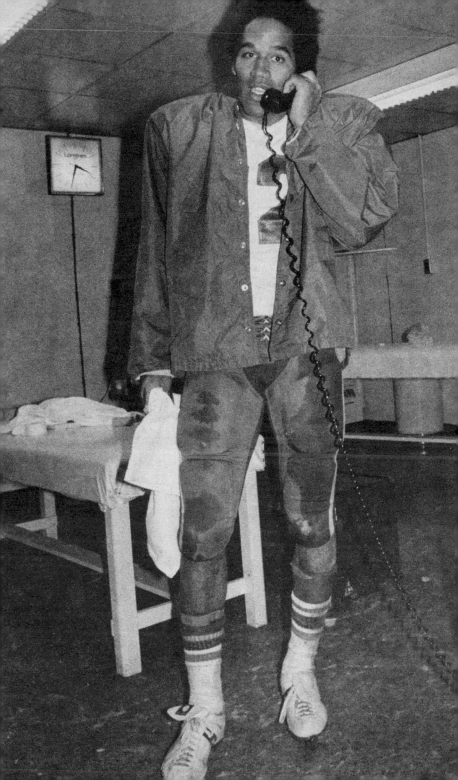

off-field jobs he wanted. He was aware that a lot of black athletes don't get the chances he was getting. But there seemed to be a special kind of magic about him.

"It may be an advantage right now for me to be black," he said. "A lot of people are out to give black people more opportunities. Five years ago it wouldn't have happened, no matter how well I played football."

O.J. was becoming a rich man even before the pro draft. He could pick and choose his opportunities. But he couldn't choose a pro team. The National Football League rules say a player has to go to the team that picks him. And the lowest team in the league always gets to pick first. O.J. wanted to stay in California. His friends were there. And he loved the warm weather. But he knew he would just have to wait.

The lowest team in the NFL in 1968 was the Buffalo Bills. So the Bills would have the first pick. Buffalo was a cold, snowy city. It was located in the East. California was in the West. If there was one place O.J. didn't want to play, it was in Buffalo.

But the Bills needed good football players, and O.J. was the best. So they picked him before any other player in the whole country. There was nothing O.J. could do. The Bills didn't want to trade him, not even for a lot of players. They wanted him in Buffalo.

It was hard for O.J. to think about playing there. He had always been the star of winning teams. And he had always played in sunny California. Now he had to go to a loser in the cold north. When the Bills asked how much money he wanted, O.J. asked for a lot.

The Buffalo club wouldn't pay him

what he first asked, so O.J. became a holdout. He refused to sign a contract, and he didn't show up for the beginning of training camp. He also missed the College All-Star Game. It wasn't until August that he finally signed.

O.J. signed a contract for four years with Buffalo. The amount of money was about $215,000. That's a lot. Off the field, he signed to work with an automobile company and a soft drink company. That would pay him a lot too. Now he didn't have to worry about money. All he had to think about was football.

He got a late start because of his holdout. The lack of practice hurt him. He didn't look as good as usual. After his first workout with the Bills, everyone was asking questions.

"Boy, am I sore," he told them.

"I'm as stiff as I've ever been. My timing is off. My body won't do the things my mind tells it to do. I guess it will take a little time to get back into shape."

A lot of people thought O.J. would have trouble with his teammates. They said the other men wouldn't like him. They would be jealous of his fame and money. But it's hard not to like O.J. Simpson. He showed them he was a hard worker. And he never acted as if he was better than his teammates. He talked and joked with all of them. And they liked him.

O.J. kept working hard in practice. He was getting into good shape. He said he'd be ready to carry the ball as much as ever.

But Coach John Rauch said he wouldn't build his attack around one man. "In the pros it's too easy for a defense to gang up on one guy," said the coach.

The Bills' quarterback Jack Kemp said the same thing. "A runner can't carry 30 times a game in the pros," said Kemp. "If a good runner gets 15 or 18 carries, he should break a couple loose. I think that's all O.J. will get. We'll also be throwing the ball to him." O.J. realized things would be different in the pros.

CHAPTER 4

O.J.'s first exhibition game was against Detroit. He didn't start, but he came in to gain 19 yards on four carries. That wasn't a bad beginning but things didn't get much better. The Bills didn't have a good offensive line. O.J. gained only 72 yards on 19 tries in the exhibitions. But he did win a starting job. He'd be in the lineup when the Bills opened the 1969 season against the New York Jets.

The Jets had a good defense and they were ready. As soon as O.J. began charging through the line the

Jets were there. They pushed the Buffalo blockers aside and hit O.J. hard. He only broke loose once, for 22 yards. The other nine times he carried he got just 13 yards in all. Wow! That surely wasn't the old O.J. And the Bills lost, 33–19.

The next week he got 19 carries against Houston. But he still didn't gain 100 yards. Then he carried 24 times against Denver. This time he got 110 yards and caught a touchdown pass. He really felt good, especially since the Bills won, 41–28.

"How sweet it is!" he yelled after the game. "I was really glad to get over 100 yards," he continued. "I should be able to do it again. I also think my blocking was getting better. I'm very happy the way things are going."

But the Bills weren't ready to give the ball to O.J. and hope for the best.

Then it was on to the pros. As a rookie, O.J. had to do a lot of watching and learning.

The team was still trying to find itself. The coaches didn't know what kind of an offense was best. In the next game O.J. got just six carries before leaving with a head injury.

He didn't play the next week. The week after that the Bills played at Oakland. O.J. was really excited. It would be his first pro game back in California. He wanted to do well. The Oakland Raiders were a tough team. It was very important for him to have a good day.

But it was not even a close game. Oakland scored the first time they had the ball. Then they scored again. Then once more. They had a big lead in the first quarter. Buffalo had to try to catch up. When a team has to catch up it usually doesn't run much. The ball gets passed instead. O.J. kept running pass patterns. But he didn't have much chance to carry the ball.

Oakland won, 50–21. And O.J. had carried just six times for 50 yards. For the first time he was very angry.

"I worked really hard for this game," he said, "but I didn't really have a chance to do anything. I just kept running out for passes and they didn't throw to me once. I'd like to be carrying the ball at least 20 times a game. I don't think that's too much to expect!"

Then he carried 10 times against Miami and only gained 12 yards. It was a terrible game for him. The Dolphin defenders didn't let him get loose. He had very little blocking. He was really taking a beating.

O.J. was disappointed. But he didn't give up. He kept trying, even when he didn't get the ball enough. He told people he thought the Bills should run more.

"All the good teams have good run-

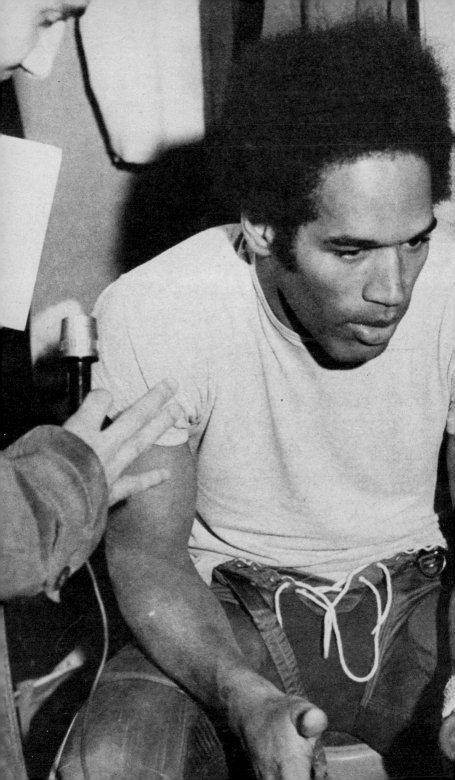

ning games," he said. "I've noticed it around the league. Look at the Jets. Joe Namath is the best passer around, but they win when the running game is going good. And Namath knows just how to use it."

The Bills won two more games late in the year. They finished with a 4–10 record. O.J. gained 697 yards on 181 tries for a 3.9 average. He scored just two touchdowns. For any other rookie that would be a good record. But for the great O.J. Simpson, it wasn't so good. Everyone had thought he'd do better. He wasn't even voted the best rookie in the league. Carl Garrett of Boston, another runner, won that prize.

"I still would like to carry the ball more," O.J. said, after the season. "That's the big thing. But I learned a lot. The hardest thing was learning the pass patterns. There are so many

After a game, the reporters come. O.J. is always friendly and talks to everyone. He is used to having microphones put in his face.

of them and I didn't run many in college.

"I was also surprised that the pro game wasn't as rough as I expected. It's not that the players aren't as tough. They are. But I was more beat up after my games at USC. I guess it's because I carried so much more there."

That's what really hurt — not getting to carry the ball. O.J. felt he was as good as any back around. He knew his blocking wasn't very good. That would have to get better. But he still wanted to run more. Maybe next year, he thought, they'll really let me carry the ball.

O.J.'s teammates all liked him. They knew he tried hard. But they also knew he didn't like playing in Buffalo. And this made them a little angry. O.J. was always flying out of town to do something else. Sometimes he was on television. Sometimes he had to get an award. Other times he had to go make TV commercials. He was very busy. And it was true that he still wished he was playing in California.

But he didn't think about that when the 1970 season started. O.J. never sulked. He wasn't the type. When he was on the field he just wanted to win. He wanted to have the best season he could. And he wanted his team to win more games.

Yet in the first game, he gained less than 50 yards though he carried 18 times. Something was really wrong. This wasn't the real O.J. Simpson. When reporters asked, O.J. said the coaches were trying to change the way he ran.

"They want me to come all the way

to the sideline on sweeps. I've always cut back as soon as there was an opening. I've got to do it my way."

But even when he ran the ball his way, O.J. couldn't gain yards without good blocking. Against the Rams O.J. gained just 24 yards on 14 carries. But once again he had no blocking.

"You can see he's a great runner," said Deacon Jones, who played end for the Rams. "If he were with us he'd gain about 2,600 yards. But by the time Buffalo gets enough good players to go with him he may be punch drunk from the beating he takes."

It was true. O.J. was really taking a beating. But he kept coming back for more. He ran a kickoff 95 yards for a TD against the Jets. He gained 127 yards against Boston. Buffalo won both games. The team had a better passing attack and was moving the

O.J. can go over them . . .

. . . Or he can go around them.

Sometimes he has to go through them.

ball. After seven games the record stood at 3–4. And O.J. was finally looking good.

Then the Bills went up against the Cincinnati Bengals. O.J. was having a good day. In the second period he ran a sweep his way. He cut back when he saw a hole and broke it for a 56-yard gain. The crowd roared. They were seeing the old O.J.

Now, just when things were going so well, O.J. had some really bad luck. He dropped back to take a kickoff. The ball came to him near the goal line and he started up field. O.J. tells what happened next.

"When I got the ball, I cut back and saw just one guy coming across the field. I was trying to set up the guy behind him when he hit me flat. He was turning my leg, trying to force me down. Because of the way he had me I was trying to go down. Then the rest of them hit me. My knee went and right away I felt it was a bad injury."

Runners fear a knee injury most of all. It can end a career. It happened to the great Gale Sayers. He had a couple of bad knee injuries and had to quit. A knee injury usually means a serious operation, too.

O.J. was helped off the field. They took him to the hospital. He was worried. The doctors had to put him to sleep with anaesthetic so they could examine the knee. O.J. said he thought he'd wake up and find they had operated. But when he awoke, a doctor said:

"Good news, O.J. We won't have to operate. The knee will heal by itself."

It *was* good news. But O.J. would miss the rest of the season. In seven games and part of one other he had gained 488 yards. He had carried 120 times. His average was up to 4.1 per

Sports stars get together. O.J. looks small next to Buffalo Braves' big basketball center Bob McAdoo.

carry. Things had been getting better. The injury came at a bad time. If he hadn't been hurt, O.J. might have had more than 200 carries and come close to 1,000 yards.

O.J.'s injury hurt the team, too. The Bills were 3–4 with O.J. Without him they didn't win again. Their final record was three wins, ten losses, and one tie (3–10–1). And after the season, Coach Rauch was replaced by Harvey Johnson. The Bills hoped 1971 would be better.

CHAPTER 5

The new coach studied his team. He said it would have a new offense.

"It's going to be O.J. left, O.J. right, and O.J. up the middle," he said. O.J. liked to hear that. It meant he would carry the ball a lot more often. He got himself back into shape. The knee healed perfectly. When 1971 started he was ready to go.

But the Bills still had problems. Players began getting hurt right from the start. Once again, O.J. didn't have blockers. Quarterback Dennis Shaw, who was very good as a rookie in

O.J.'s foot got hurt. He's temporarily out of the action.

1970, was having trouble. The first game was against Dallas. The Cowboys have a very good defense. They jumped all over O.J. He gained just 25 yards on 14 carries. That's less than two yards a try. He went nowhere.

In his next two games O.J. gained 82 and 45 yards, but the Bills lost both games. They were 0–3. O.J. was hardly carrying at all. The team looked terrible. They played Baltimore and were beaten, 43–0. O.J. carried just seven times and actually *lost* 10 yards. It was unreal.

O.J. was hurt and embarrassed. And angry, too. He was playing with the worst team in the league.

"The team played a terrible game," he said, "the worst since I've been here. We had receivers open, but how can the quarterback throw when he's flat on his back. I don't know what I'm going to do. I've just got to try not to go crazy."

The team won just one game all year. There were rumors that O.J. wanted to leave Buffalo. He had only one 100-yard day all year, 106 against San Diego. When the season ended he had gained 742 yards on 183 carries, a 4.1 average. It was the old story. How much more could O.J. take?

Then he got some good news. The Bills were getting another coach. He was Lou Saban, who had coached the team in the early 1960's. The Bills had been winners then. Saban had then moved to Denver. Now he was coming back to Buffalo. O.J. didn't know Saban. But he knew one thing. Coach Saban liked to run the football.

"I'm very happy that Lou Saban is coming here," said O.J. "He's just the guy to turn the team around. As for me, I'm down now, but believe me,

I'm gonna get back up there. I came out of USC as a running back. But I haven't had the chances that some other pro runners have had. They carry the ball maybe 100 times more than I do in a year. With Coach Saban coming, I hope things will change."

O.J. really believed in Lou Saban. He decided to sign a new contract with Buffalo. He still liked California, better than Buffalo, New York, but he was loyal to his team. He wanted to stay and help them become winners.

"I've cried a lot with these guys," he said. "Now I want to stay around and drink champagne with them." (If the Bills won the championship, they would drink champagne to celebrate.)

O.J. was right about Lou Saban. When training camp started in 1972, the coach got his offensive linemen together. Then he pointed at O.J.

"See that number '32' over there,"

Saban said. "You guys give him some blocking and he'll put bread and butter on your tables."

Saban knew that O.J. could be the best runner in the league if he had the chance. He wanted to give him that chance.

And O.J. wanted to get it. He took his weight down from 215 pounds to 205, so he would be faster. And he was in great shape. He said he wanted to gain 1,500 yards. He had been without a great season for three years and he wanted a comeback.

The Bills lost their first game and O.J. didn't do very well. People were beginning to lose faith in him. Then the Bills played San Francisco and the real O.J. Simpson came back.

O.J. was the main man in the attack. He kept carrying up the middle and around the ends. They gave him the ball three, four, five times in a row. It was like college again. And The Juice was performing well. He was breaking tackles, faking and outrunning defenders. When the game ended, Buffalo had won, 27–20, and O.J. was the star. He had 138 yards on 29 carries. That was more like it.

"This has got to be my greatest thrill in pro football," he said. "When I was a kid I'd watch John Brodie and the 49ers play at Kezar Stadium. Now I'm playing against them and we beat them."

It was about time O.J. tasted some of the glory in pro ball. He had waited a long time. But he didn't want to get too high just because of one good game. Now he had to prove himself the rest of the season. At least he knew he'd finally get the chance.

Now O.J. really began to run. Two weeks after one 49ers game, he ran through the tough Oakland defense for 144 yards on 28 carries. Not many backs do that to the Raiders. The Bills lost the game, but thanks to O.J., it was close.

There were more injuries on the offensive line, but this time nothing stopped the Juice. He was getting the ball more and if he got just the smallest block, he was gone. Playing before the home fans in a game with the Steelers, O.J. really went wild. Early in the game he took a pitchout at his own six. Twisting his way through the line he then made a nifty cut, pushed another tackler aside, and took off.

He outran the rest of the Steelers and galloped 94 yards for a TD. It was the longest run of the entire NFL season. When that game ended he had 189 yards, the best day of his career. O.J. was again showing how good he was. How very god.

The rest of the year was more of the

Soon O.J. learned to get away on his own, using his speed and his "moves."

O.J. is so quick, defenders end up grabbing air.

same. Against New England he made a great, 13-yard TD-run to win the game in the final minutes. He had 103 yards that day. Then he got 116 in a tie game with tough Detroit. When he ran for 93 yards against Cleveland in the 11th game he went over the 1,000 yard mark. He had finally done it.

But he wasn't through yet. He got 101 against the Redskins and ended with 1,251 yards on 292 carries for a 4.3 average. (Only Ron Johnson of the Giants had more carries.) O.J. was the leading runner in the league. He had his wish. And the future looked good.

"We lost five guards, a center, and a tackle during the year," said a Bills' coach. "So O.J. made a lot of yards on his own. Each lineman blocks differently, so it was hard for O.J. to really get his rhythm with them. But he didn't quit. If we'd stayed healthy he'd have had 1,500 yards."

O.J. played in the Pro Bowl game that year. That's the game between the NFC and AFC (National and American Football Conferences). The game has the best players in the league. And he was the best player on the field. He gained 122 yards on just 16 carries. He scored one touchdown and caught three passes for 58 yards. He was named the Outstanding Player of the Game, and led his team to a 33–28 victory. For the first time in his pro career he was anxious for the next year to start.

CHAPTER 6

During the off-season, O.J. was still very busy. He was on television very often and traveled a great deal. Yet he worked-out every day without fail.

"A runner will go only as far as his legs take him," he said. "I run every day. I do a lot of sprints, back and forth. I keep my legs in top shape all year round. It's not wise to let them go in the off-season and then try to get in shape at camp. You should be in top shape at camp so you can concentrate on other things, like getting your game rhythm and working with your blockers."

Blockers. That was a key word. Saban had rebuilt the offensive line. Now, if there were no injuries, O.J. would have really good blocking for the first time. There was a young guard named Reggie McKenzie who was outstanding. He loved leading O.J. on sweeps and traps. O.J. called him in the off-season and said he'd like to get 1,600 yards in '73. McKenzie listened, then said:

"Why not make it 2,000!"

"Why not," said O.J.

When the season started, O.J. and McKenzie, and the rest of the team were ready. There was a new quarterback, Joe Ferguson of Arkansas, and two good fullbacks, Jim Braxton and Larry Watkins. There were also good receivers in J.D. Hill and Bob Chandler. O.J. finally had a decent team around him.

The first game was against the New

74   O.J. looks to the open field after making one of his quick cuts.

The Bills' blocking improved. Here, O.J.
follows tackle Willie Young (68) on a sweep.

O.J. and his favorite blocker Reggie McKenzie (67),
after another Buffalo victory.

England Patriots. O.J. got the ball on the first play of the game. He made a good gain. He got the ball again. Another good gain. He looked fast and confident. He was running hard and well. He kept getting the ball and gaining yards.

It wasn't long before he broke one, showing his great moves. He got two blocks at the line, and was off. He ran 80 yards for a touchdown and Buffalo had the lead. Later he ran 22 yards for another score.

In the fourth quarter the Bills were way ahead and O.J. was over 200 yards. He had a chance to break the record for yards gained in a single game. The record was 247 yards, set by Willie Ellison of Los Angeles. So The Juice kept going. With a little more than a minute left he ran off-tackle for seven yards. That gave him 250 yards on 29 carries. It was a new record. And Buffalo won the game, 31–13.

"He looked like Grant going through Richmond," said New England coach Chuck Fairbanks. "We were helpless. We couldn't slow him down. We'd have a hole blocked up, but O.J.'s natural ability would get him away."

Linebacker Edgar Chandler was tired out from trying to tackle O.J.

"He's even faster than he looks," said Chandler. "You think you have the angle on him, then suddenly he's gone. It was really embarrassing."

O.J., was very happy. And he was glad to have good blocking at last.

"I don't think anyone will criticize our line again," he said. "They were just blowing the other guys out. They've been telling me they're going to get me 1,700 yards this year. Well,

Everyone wants O.J.'s picture. Sometimes they had to work pretty hard to get it.

they're sure playing as if they mean it."

Whenever O.J. ran for a good gain, he thanked his offensive line. He's that kind of guy. He knows it takes teamwork to win. One man can't do it alone. O.J. had been trying that for three years. So he praised his blockers and kept telling them how good they were.

He got 103 yards the next week, then 123 against the Jets the week after that. Jet linebacker Ralph Baker talked about trying to tackle O.J.

"It seems that everything on him moves," said Baker. "He moves his head, he moves his hips, he moves his legs, he moves his shoulders. A lot of times I knew where the play was coming and I could get the angle. But then you still have to tackle him. And no one can do it alone."

The Simpson express was really

80   O.J. loves to run against the New England Patriots. He gained 250 yards against them in the first game of the 1973 season.

rolling. He had 171 yards against Philadelphia and 166 against Baltimore. After a 55-yard day with Miami, he came back for 157 against Kansas City. People began saying he might break the record. The record was 1,863 yards in one year. It was held by the great Jim Brown. A lot of people thought it would never be broken. But O.J. had a chance. And to make it even better, the Bills were winning games.

Once again the whole country was asking the question. "How many yards did O.J. get?" It had been a long time. People liked O.J. Most of them wanted him to break the record. Even the players on the other teams liked him. He always gave credit to others. He was always friendly to reporters and writers. He never acted cocky or stuck up. His college coach,

After the Patriots game, O.J. gets a handshake from Ralph Wilson, the owner of the Buffalo Bills.

John McKay, spoke for a lot of people.

"O.J. isn't only the finest player I've ever coached," McKay said, "but he's the finest human being as well."

And his pro coach, Lou Saban, said: "You don't find many like him. He's a man, a great team man."

So everyone watched as O.J. ran. He gained 79 yards against New Orleans and 99 against Cincinnati. Then he ran past Miami for 120, Baltimore for 124, and Atlanta for 137. But it still wasn't enough. To break the record he would have to get almost 300 yards in his final two games.

It was a cold, snowy day in New England. The Bills were playing the Patriots. The field was very slippery. Most backs can't run very well on that kind of field. But O.J. is a very special back. He ran and ran, while the others slipped. When the game ended

84   That 1973 season. Before the last game against the New York Jets, O.J. has a few moments alone to think about breaking the record.

Off and flying. In the Jets game, snow was
falling, but the blocking was great. O.J. and
his teammates broke Jim Brown's record in
the very first quarter.

he had 219 yards on just 22 carries. That made his total 1,803. He needed just 61 yards against the Jets to break the record.

The whole football world watched Shea Stadium in New York on a cold December day in 1973. The huge crowd screamed from the beginning. And the Juice went to work.

He was banging it out right from the start. Buffalo took the opening kickoff and marched 71 yards in 12 plays for a TD. O.J. carried on seven of those plays and gained 57 yards. He needed only four more.

The next time the Bills got the ball they gave it right to O.J. He got a block from his fullback, Jim Braxton, and plowed through left tackle for six yards. He had broken the record. His teammates mobbed around him. They gave him the football to keep. He had done it!

This is the final run in the game against the Jets. It gave O.J. 2,003 yards for the season—a record that may never be broken unless O.J. breaks it himself.

After the record, O.J. gets a hug from his coach, Lou Saban.

O.J. faces the reporters for the last time in the 1973 season. As usual, O.J. gave his teammates a lot of credit. It was a great end to a great season.

Whenever someone asked O.J. about the record he never said "I." He always said "we," because he thought it was as much his teammates' as his own. And his teammates had played extra well.

But O.J. wasn't finished. He went back in and kept running. Now 2,000 yards was the goal. The Bills were really rolling. They were playing like champs. O.J. had carried more than any player in history. But he didn't seem tired. He seemed as good as the first day of the year.

His last carry came in the snowy, grey final minutes. He gained seven more yards for 2,003 on the year. The Bills won, 34–14, to finish with a 9–5 record.

Once again O.J. was mobbed. McKenzie had his hands in the air in victory. O.J. hugged his all-pro guard.

Relax, O.J. You've earned it!

After the game, O.J. was happy it was over. He was glad to relax.

"There was a lot of pressure on me," he said. "It kept building up. I had a tough time sleeping this week. But the guys were great. They kept saying they'd get it for me. And they did. Without this great bunch of guys I couldn't have done it. Believe me."

So it was over. There was the one-game record, the one-year record, the carry record, the 200-yard record. And the Bills broke the Dolphins' team-rushing record. It was hard to believe that this was the Buffalo team of two years earlier, when O.J. was ready to play somewhere else. Now he is a Bill. He says he'll stay in Buffalo until he retires.

O.J. Simpson has known bad times as well as good times. He's a man who never quits, who never gives up. He believes that hard work will get him